MY FIRST LOOK AT PLANETS

SATURN IS A BIG, SMOOTH, RINGED PLANET

Saturn

TERESA WIMMER

CREATIVE EDUCATION

Published by Creative Education

P.O. Box 227, Mankato, Minnesota 56002

Creative Education is an imprint of The Creative Company

Designed by Rita Marshall

Photographs by Getty Images (The Image Bank, Photonica), Photo Researchers (Julian

Baum / Science Photo Library, Chris Butler / Science Photo Library, Lynette Cook / Science

Photo Library, David Ducros / Science Photo Library, Library of Congress / Science Source,

Steve Munsinger, NASA / Mark Marten, Science Photo Library, U.S. Department of Energy /

Science Photo Library), Tom Stack & Associates (JPL / TSADO, TSADO / NASA)

Copyright © 2008 Creative Education

Printed in the United States of America

Library of Congress Cataloging-in-Publication Data

Wimmer, Teresa, 1975- Saturn / by Teresa Wimmer.

p. cm. — (My first look at planets)

Includes index.

ISBN-13: 978-1-58341-522-1

1. Saturn (Planet)—Juvenile literature. I. Title.

QB671.W73 2007   523.46—dc22   2006018253

First edition 9 8 7 6 5 4 3 2 1

SATURN

Big and Bright 6

Cold, Stormy, and Fast 8

Rings and Moons 12

More to Learn 16

Hands-On: Make a Planet Saturn 22

Additional Information 24

Big and Bright

A long time ago, people looked up at the night sky. They saw a small, bright ball far away. Every night the ball was in a different place. People thought it was a moving star. But it was really the **planet** Saturn.

Saturn is part of the **solar system**. Besides Saturn, there are seven other planets. All of the planets move in a path called an orbit

SATURN (TOP LEFT) IS ONE OF EIGHT PLANETS

around the sun. Saturn is the sixth planet from the sun.

Saturn is the second-biggest planet. It is made of **gas** and liquid. There is no ground on Saturn. If people went there, they would sink down through the gas.

COLD, STORMY, AND FAST

Saturn is far away from the sun's heat. That makes it a very cold place. Sometimes strong winds blow across Saturn. Big storms

Saturday is a day of the week on Earth. Saturday and Saturn were named after a god called Saturn.

Saturn spins like a top in the sky. It never stops spinning. Saturn is not very heavy. That means it spins very fast.

RINGS AND MOONS

Up close, Saturn looks yellow. It is very pretty. Many bright rings circle Saturn. They are made of chunks of rock and ice. The rings look orange and red. Some rings are broken. Some are braided like a girl's hair.

Saturn's rings have different chunks. Some chunks are as small as pebbles. Some are as big as houses.

SATURN HAS THE BIGGEST RINGS OF ANY PLANET

Saturn also has at least 46 moons. They move in an orbit around Saturn. Some of the moons are very big. The biggest moon is named Titan. It looks like a big, orange ball of ice.

Some of Saturn's moons are as small as a football field. They are called "shepherd moons." They move in Saturn's rings.

SATURN'S BIGGEST MOONS ARE OUTSIDE ITS RINGS

MORE TO LEARN

Saturn is the most faraway planet people can see with just their eyes. They use a **telescope** to see more about the planet.

People have sent **probes** to Saturn, too. The probes have special cameras that take pictures of Saturn up close. Some probes' cameras have taken pretty pictures of Saturn's rings. Others have found more moons near Saturn.

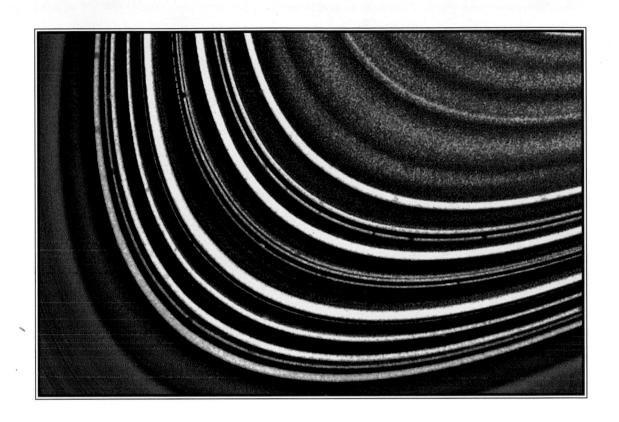

Saturn's rings are always changing shape. People think the rings might even go away someday!

PROBES' PICTURES HELP PEOPLE STUDY SATURN'S RINGS

THERE ARE GAPS BETWEEN SOME OF SATURN'S RINGS

Not long ago, another probe went to Saturn. It landed on the moon Titan. It will stay there for four years. Pictures from the probe are being sent back to people on Earth. Each picture shows something new about Saturn!

THE *CASSINI* SPACESHIP CARRIED A PROBE TO TITAN

Hands-on: Make a Planet Saturn

Saturn is a pretty planet. You can make your very own planet Saturn!

What You Need

A big Styrofoam ball

A piece of yarn about eight inches (20 cm) long

A yellow marker

Two orange, two yellow, and two red pipe cleaners

Glue

What You Do

1. Color the Styrofoam ball yellow.
2. Glue the red pipe cleaners around the middle of the ball. Glue the orange pipe cleaners on top of the red ones. Glue the yellow pipe cleaners on top of the orange ones.
3. Glue one end of the yarn to the top of the ball.
4. Now you have your own planet Saturn!

SATURN IS WELL-KNOWN FOR ITS BRIGHT RINGS

INDEX

color 12

gas 8, 10

moons 14, 16, 20

probes 16, 20

rings 12, 13, 14, 16, 17

size 8, 12

solar system 6

storms 8, 10

sun 8

WORDS TO KNOW

gas—a kind of air; some gases are harmful to breathe

planet—a round object that moves around the sun

probes—special machines that fly around or land on a planet or a moon

solar system—the sun, the planets, and their moons

telescope—a special tube that people look through to see faraway things up close

READ MORE

Rudy, Lisa Jo. *Planets!* New York: HarperCollins, 2005.

Taylor-Butler, Christine. *Saturn.* New York: Scholastic, 2005.

Vogt, Gregory. *Solar System.* New York: Scholastic, 2001.

EXPLORE THE WEB

Enchanted Learning: Saturn http://www.zoomschool.com/subjects/astronomy/
planets/saturn

Funschool: Space http://funschool.kaboose.com/globe-rider/space/
index.html?trnstl=1

StarChild: The Planet Saturn http://starchild.gsfc.nasa.gov/docs/StarChild/
solar_system_level1/saturn.html